WHY THE WORST SINNERS MAKE THE BEST SAINTS

WHEN SIN IS GRACE
WHEN GRACE IS SIN

By Michael Lister

The Song of Suffering: Meditations from Job
The Resurrection and other Stories of Love

WHY THE WORST **SINNERS** MAKE THE BEST **SAINTS**

WHEN SIN IS GRACE
WHEN GRACE IS SIN

Michael Lister

ST. MATTHEW'S PRESS
P.O. BOX 1130
WEWAHITCHKA, FL 32465
904-639-3700

WHY THE WORST SINNERS
MAKE THE BEST SAINTS
When Sin is Grace / When Grace is Sin
Copyright 1995 by Michael Lister. All rights reserved. Printed in the United States.

First St. Matthew's Press Paperback edition: February 11, 1996 - the author's 28th birthday.

ISBN: 1888146-00-1

Library of Congress Catalog Card Number: 95-72160

1 3 5 7 9 10 8 6 4 2

Printed in the USA by

Morris Publishing

3212 E. Hwy 30
Kearney, NE 68847
800-650-7888

For the love of my life

and too, this time,
for Richard Gaydos,
who taught me of God's grace
and
Grace Kelly,
a grace for us all.

But where sin increased,
grace increased all the more.

Shall we go on sinning so
that grace might increase?

ACKNOWLEDGMENTS

Why the worst Sinners make the best Saints and its author owes special thanks to the following:

To Pam - I don't have the words, and I'm supposed to be a writer.

To Bobbie Palmer, Eddie Merritt, Pam Lister, Rick & Barbara Wyatt for faithfulness above and beyond the call of duty.

To Mike and Judi Lister for giving me a lifetime's supply of life lessons relating to grace.

To Meleah and Micah, who themselves are God's grace in my life.

To Father Andrew M. Greeley for his masterful novel on God's grace - *An Occasion of Sin.*

To Frederick Buechner - a real writer, whose use of words is evidence of God's grace.

To Helen Carlsten and Lori Price for all of the support, encouragement, and proof reading.

To Aron Myers for the truest friendship, and all of the extraordinary Negro Spiritual inspiration too.

To all those who have at one time or another and in one way or another discipled me: Mike & Judi Lister, Gladys Mcknight, Fatima Barry, John Milton Whitfield Sr., Clarence Pape, Joel Smith, and Pastors Jim Fillingjim, David and Judy Warren, Zane Jones, Gary Stenson, Earl and Don Paulk, Jim Oborne, Dan Rhodes, Steve Hodges, Bob Blackwood, Kirby Clemments, Pete Aycock.

WARNING:
This book contains a little (very little) profanity.

As a minister and teacher, I have struggled with the issue of whether or not to use profanity when writing, the following is the result of that struggle.

When I write I try to, above all else, be honest. Being honest as a writer includes a great deal of self disclosure - I tell my secrets, I confess my sins. In addition, I try and let my characters be honest too. When I write fiction, I do not create characters as much as allow them to emerge. And, as they do, some of them, like many of their real life counterparts, use profanity. Part of my being honest and having integrity as a writer comes from allowing my characters to speak in their voice and to use their language. I attempt to censor them as little as possible (though I do censor them a great deal), even when they use language that I do not, or commit deeds that I do not. If their language offends you, I am sorry, that is not its intent. It is just that I can think of no other way to write modern fiction than to allow my modern characters to speak and act the way modern people do. Therefore, in the worlds that I create, I allow people to say pretty much whatever they wish, just like God does in his.

CONTENTS

Introduction	11
The Nature of Sin	13
The Wages of Sin	19
The Measure of a Sin	29
Daddy's Angel	33
Beyond the Law	39
Physician, Heal Thy Son	43
When Sin is Grace	53
The Prodigal Son	59
Seven Steps from Sin to Grace	65
The Nature of Grace	75
The Purpose of Grace	79
Too Much of a Good Thing	83
When Grace is Sin	89
Why Sinners make Saints	95

INTRODUCTION

What follows is an experiment. It is my first attempt to combine fiction and nonfiction in one book. The result is ... well, the verdict is still out on that one. There is a truth that, I believe, cannot be gotten at in any other way than in a story. So, rather than merely telling you all that I want to, I hope to show you as well. And, I hope that the stories do just that - show. I also hope that the nonfiction chapters do just the other - tell. The result of which, I hope, will ultimately be good communication. Is it? I think so, but yours is the opinion that counts. Let me know what you think.

Through the showing and the telling of this book, I hope that you come to truth. That is to say, I hope you come to the specific truth about sin and grace and, more generally - THE TRUTH. Know what (or rather Who) I mean? THE TRUTH is **LOVE**, which is directly related to the part of the truth that this book is all about - **GRACE**. The truth of God's grace is as astounding as anything I have ever heard in the world of fact or fiction. It is truly amazing.

God's grace is also life-changing. And, while I know that this book is not life-changing, I do hope and pray that, by God's grace, it becomes a vehicle for change in your life - particularly in the area of grace and sin. If I have one message, and I hope that it comes across in this book, it is that God's incredible love for you is far more than you can ever know or understand. Reach out for that love - embrace it, possess it, and most importantly, be possessed by it.

The painting on the cover is Sandro Botticelli's *The Lamentation* (1490). I chose it after a lengthy search and much deliberation. I really like it. Of all the sinners who have become saints, Mary Magdalen most embodies what this book is all about. She was utterly and irrevocably changed by grace. When she met Jesus, her occasion of sin was transformed into an occasion of grace. From that moment on, she has been instrumental both as a symbol and metaphor of God's amazing grace.

THE NATURE OF SIN

As with most things, much of the nature of sin remains a mystery to me. If I understand sin at all, it is at its most elementary level. My best understanding of sin has come not so much from my study of it, but more from my personal struggles with it. I am a sinner. I may not know much about sin, but I do know that throughout my life I have sinned and that I continue to sin until this very day. Therefore, my comments on the nature of sin will be both limited and autobiographical and should not be viewed as a complete biblical discourse on the concept of sin.

We are not told specifically how sin entered the universe. However, it does appear that long before Adam and Eve's sin in the Garden of Eden, sin existed in the world already. Of course, this raises many questions about the nature of God, his creation, and the role of sin in it. Did God create sin, or did he merely create a world in which there was the possibility of sin? Could it be that the answer to those two questions are one and the same? Was sin, or at least the possibility of sin, vital to the creation of the world that God willed into existence?

The answer to each of the above questions is the same - "I don't know." I am sure that there are people who are convinced that they know those answers and perhaps they do. However, I must be honest with you regarding the nature of my limitations and lack of knowledge, wisdom, and understanding. My honest feeling, though, is that it is the intent of the Bible to leave many questions unanswered and several mysteries unsolved about much of its content, including sin.

Therefore, any teaching on sin that claims to be complete must include conjecture on the part of the teacher. I am not saying, however, that conjecture is wrong, just that we must see it for what it is - a shot in the dark, or at best, an educated guess. Thus, my answer to where did sin come from is, "I don't know." However, as to the question of whether or not sin really exists my answer is a definitive, "Yes, it does." How do I know? Because I am chief among sinners.

Without knowing exactly how sin came into existence, we are told how it came to be a human condition - through Adam, the first human. However, do not be too hard on ol' Adam, because if he hadn't done it, one of us most certainly would have. Sin entered the realm of humanity through the temptation to be like God and the choice to disobey God's command regarding the fruit of the tree. And, we have been craving forbidden fruit ever since, even though the fruit from the tree of life is just as accessible to us. This, to me, best describes our human condition - we have access to both life and death, but there is something in our nature (sin) that longs for the forbidden.

Some people have attempted to reduce sin to simply the consequences of making bad choices. However, the confession of St. Paul refutes this when he says, "What I want to do I do not do, but what I hate I do. I desire to do what is good, but I cannot carry it out." Sin is a sickness. Sin has a nature. Sin is a powerful force that we would do well not to underestimate. Sin is a part of our humanity.

As you might well imagine, there are many definitions of sin in the Bible. The mystical and ambiguous nature of sin makes it difficult to define, thus, there have been many attempts. We can, perhaps, get a balanced view of sin by that which emerges from the collective biblical conceptualizations.

Sin has been defined as a missing of the mark or a deviation from the goal. It is also seen as the deviation of the moral norm (the law or will of God). Going astray or wandering about like lost sheep and stumbling around like a drunk man are also concepts related to sin. Sin also embodies the concept of rebellion. It is the defiance of the holy lordship of God. Deliberate perversion or twisting of truth is also sin. Another definition for sin is ignorance, as in being unwilling to learn or to be enlightened because of a closed mind or a hard heart. Inattention, as in hearing amiss or incorrectly or failing to acknowledge what has been made obvious is sin as well. Finally, sin is all wrong doing. Everything that is evil, in error, twisted, wicked, or wrong is sin.

To the above concepts of sin must be added the most common characteristic of sin. Sin always involves God. Just as without God there could be no sin, sin is an action against God. Whether it is a thought, a word, or a deed, sin is ultimately an act against God. Sin is that which contradicts God - who he is, what he says, and what he does. And though sin is manifest in many different ways and against many different people, it is always, at least indirectly, an act committed against God.

Sin is the displacement of God. It is the failure to let God be God. When we place ourselves or anyone or anything above or before God, we have sinned. Idolatry is a very common sin in most of our lives because of our need for the tangible and our need to control. When you and I displace God with ourselves, our ideas, others, or things, we are committing sin.

Sin also involves a violation of the command to love. Love cannot sin. When we are motivated by love and when we act in love we cannot sin. Not only does love cover a multitude of sin, but also where true love is there is no place for sin. When we sin, we are acting in a way that is less than loving. This ranges from abuse to over-indulgence and everything in between, but sin occurs when we do not act out of love.

The consequences of sin are, I believe, rather obvious. First, there is the devastation of relationships. The relationship between God and man and between man and man has been forever changed by sin. Sin replaces love in relationships with shame, fear, selfishness, dependency, envy, hate, abuse, faithlessness, distrust, and indifference. An obvious strain exists in even the best of relationships - this is the result of sin.

Sin is separation. Anything that separates us from God and one another is sin. Sin drives a wedge between all relationships. In its centrifugal force, sin spins everything outward away from the center and away from wholeness. We are driven from unity and oneness by sin. We are alone and lonely because of the power of sin to separate.

Sin prevents us from truly being who we are and who we were created to be. Because sin causes us to lose our identity and our freedom, it takes away from our humanity and our hope for divinity. Adam and Eve, after sinning, no longer felt comfortable with who they were - they covered themselves and hid. Sin causes us to fail to reach our potential because it causes us to wander about aimlessly like lost sheep and people high on drugs or alcohol.

Another consequence of sin is the fall of creation. We are told that sin threw the workings of nature out of balance. Natural disasters, failed crops, fruitless ground, and thorns and thistles are all the result of sin. All of creation groans under the weight of the curse and the hope for redemption. Disharmony among the forces of nature, like the disharmony between mankind, is the result of sin.

Sin brings unproductive pain and suffering. "*The way of a transgressor is hard,*" is how the Bible says that sin brings trouble. Whether it's fear of the husband of the woman you are having an affair with, the anxiety caused by trying to remember which lie you told which person, or the dread of the creditor's phone call, sin causes hardship. Sin causes worry, fear, depression, anxiety, stress, panic, and restlessness. The hardship of sin makes the yoke of Christ all the more appealing.

Perhaps the most devastating of all of the results of sin is its gravest consequence - death. The wages of sin are death. Death entered the world through sin. Sin has a penalty. Though usually payed on a deferred payment plan, sin is never without the highest of prices. Sin brings death - spiritual, emotional, psychological, sexual, intellectual, and finally physical death. You and I are going to die - that's a fact, and that fact exists because of sin.

Every bad, wicked, evil, cruel, degrading, unholy thing in existence is a product and symptom of sin. Sin is with us, among us, and in us. We are sinners. We have been infested with sin, it is our heritage, our birthright, a part of our nature.

THE WAGES OF SIN
a story

He sat alone in his room amidst his trophies of war. "*His room*" was actually a spare bedroom that he had converted into an office, which in reality was more of an arsenal. He was, after all, a soldier. He sat there, outwardly anyway, cleaning his Glock nine millimeter with the precision and care required for such a fine weapon, while inwardly he was tormented with familiar, yet terrifying thoughts. Though tortured, he remained calm, due in part to his unique training, due in part to his being in his room - the only room in their house in which he felt at home. The "*their*," of their house, was his wife, Sandy and their son, or perhaps her son (he wasn't sure), Shane. In other parts of their house hung pictures of the happy family - Stephen, Sandy, and Shane. However, none were to be found in his office, because they were not a happy family, if they were a family at all. This inner sanctum of his displayed many things: marksman trophies, medals, awards, and the heads of stuffed animals from distant hunts, but only one picture was displayed. The picture was matted and framed to match the room and was of his father and him on a hunting trip they had taken when he was still a boy. In the picture he was grinning from ear to ear, and why shouldn't he have been, it was the happiest day of his life - he had just killed his first buck.

    He knew that the man pictured with him was his father. He did not know, however, if the boy pictured with him in the other rooms of the house was his son, and this tormented him day and night. After his own father had been killed when he was only fourteen, he had longed to have a son of his own to share the great hunting experiences with, and everything else, too. He had longed for a son for so many years, and now that he finally had one, he was unsure if he really did, in fact, have one. Of course, his wife had reassured him that Shane was his son, but how was he supposed to believe a lying whore. Shane was five years old and for five long years he had wondered, but now he did more than wonder, he suspected.

    Shane had been born during a previous era in

Stephen's life. An era in which he, a young Navy lieutenant, nailed everything with a pulse. He had long since forgotten how many women he had been with, but it was in the hundreds during his long and distinguished career. He wasn't sure why he did it. He actually never gave it much thought, especially now that he was essentially monogamous. If it were true that there were wages for sin, he was paying top prices. He often thought that hell would be a much welcomed relief compared to his present torment. The torment and price of his sin was the result of Sandy finding him with woman after woman and swearing to take revenge. She swore that she would soon sleep with everybody on the Navy base, starting with his friend and boss Captain William (Bill) Waterford. Stephen never knew if she ever honored her pledge, but the older Shane grew the more he thought he could see Bill in him.

As he continued to care for, almost caress, the weapon in his hands, he heard the front door open and Sandy and Shane come in. He braced himself, for he knew that at any minute they would both enter his door, breaking the parameter of his fortress. He listened as their foot falls got closer and closer, until finally there were two small knocks on the door followed by Sandy opening the door and walking in.

"This came for you today," she said as she tossed the latest edition of *Handgun* magazine on the footlocker that doubled as his coffee table. No warmth and barely any civility could be detected in her voice. Since his obsession had escalated, she had become increasingly distant.

"Thanks," he said without looking up.

Just then, Shane ran in past his mother and over to the desk where his dad sat cleaning his gun. Ignoring the repeated rebukes he had received in the past, he pulled the clip from the desktop.

"Hey, daddy, are you cleaning the clock?" he asked.

"Don't grab that," Stephen responded to him as he snatched the clip from the boy's small hand. "That is very dangerous. Never, never touch any of this stuff, understand? Guns kill. They are not toys. And, it's a Glock. A GLOCK, not a clock. How many times am I going to have to tell you that?"

"Daddy, when are you going to teach me how to shoot?" Shane asked, not in the least dissuaded by his dad's rebuke. "Tommy's daddy taught him to shoot."

"You're not old enough yet."

"But Tommy's daddy. . . ."

"Tommy's dad is an idiot. Anyway, I said no."

"Yes, sir," Shane said dropping his head and beginning to back away.

"Come on, son," Sandy said, "let's go get a snack and watch some 'toons."

"Yes, ma'am. Bye-bye lieutenant," Shane said, and gave a small salute before he turned to leave.

"Hey," Stephen said.

"Yes, sir," Shane said as he turned back around, hope rising in his heart at the possibility of his dad asking him to stay .

"Don't be a smart ass."

"No, sir. I wasn't sir," he said, his eyes beginning to well up with tears.

"He needs more discipline in his life," Stephen yelled to Sandy, but got no reply.

"I'm just practicing because I want to be a soldier like you and Uncle Bill."

"Uncle Bill? Who told you to call him Uncle Bill?"

"He did, and mommy said it was alright."

"When did you see Captain Waterford?"

"The other day."

Stephen knew that the "*Other day,*" could mean anything from yesterday to a week ago, when Shane said it. In fact, it could have actually meant earlier the same day.

"Okay, I've got work to do. Go in there with your mother."

"Yes, sir. Can I come and help you in a little while?"

"No, not today. I've got too much work to do and you'd just get in the way. Besides, you're too young."

Shane started to leave again, and again Stephen

stopped him.

"Hey, wait a minute," Stephen called to Shane as he noticed a piece of cotton under a Band-Aid on Shane's upper right arm.

Shane quickly turned around and came back with no sign of exasperation, because any attention, even harassment, was better than no attention at all.

"What is that on your arm," Stephen asked.

"That's where I got my shot."

"Your shot?"

"Yes sir. Uncle Bill and I got one together."

"What kind of shot?"

"Blood shot."

"They took blood out of your and Captain Waterford's arm," Stephen asked, lividly.

"Yes sir, and I was a very brave boy. Like a soldier, Uncle Bill said."

"Dismissed."

"Sir?"

"Go in there with your mother - now!"

Shane ran out as fast as he could, sensing that his dad was mad at him again. He knew what would happen to him if he stayed any longer.

Stephen stood and began to pace the floor of his room. The room that he loved. The room where the walls had suddenly begun coming in on him. He plotted and planned. Rage serged through his body like power serges in an electrical storm. Inside he was a storm. Outside, however, he was seemingly calm. The calm before the storm. He decided to go for a ride to clear his head - to sort things out - to finalize his plans.

As he drove around, much faster than he should have, Stephen thought about all the hopes and dreams he had placed in having a son. He cried. Stephen was not an uncaring or unfeeling man. On the contrary, he had much love to give to a son of his own. In fact, that was what made this all the more painful. Stephen was not acting like himself and he knew it, but he felt as if he could do nothing to change.

When he got back home, he headed straight to his room. His wife was waiting there for him.

"Where the hell have you been?"

He didn't reply. He just starred.

"Steve, what's going on? You left your gun out on the table and your door open."

He thought for a moment, searching his mind for the perfect response. When he had found the one that would draw blood he said, "I thought you might want to use it."

"You son of a bitch. God, you are so cold. Listen, I don't know how much more of this I can take," she said, and with that sunk down to the couch like a balloon with a slow leak having just lost the last of its air.

"There's the door. Close it on your way out. And I'm sure that Bill's door stands open for you."

"What the hell is wrong with you? Bill is a happily married man, and you know it."

"Maybe, but you sure as hell didn't say that you wouldn't go back to him."

"What do you mean go *back* to him?"

"You know exactly what I mean."

"What did he say to you?"

With that single question she confirmed all of his fears. He walked over to where she was seated on the couch, pulled her off of it, and slapped her hard across the face. She fell back on the couch and began to cry. The look on her face was pure horror and confusion, and pain too. He had never hit her before, but she had never ruined his life before either.

She slowly got up after a few minutes and carefully walked out, keeping her back to the wall and her eyes on this stranger, her husband, the whole way. When she reached the door she felt almost safe again, due in part to his being seated. His whole demeanor changed. He now looked depressed and lethargic.

"Why?" Was all she could manage to get out, and that only in a whisper.

"That's the way whores are treated," he said barely above a whisper himself and without looking up. "And I hate you for bringing all of this shit out of me. You have robbed me of the one thing that I ever really wanted."

She closed the door and walked away. He again spent the night on the couch in his room.

The next morning he was up bright and early doing reloads and polishing blue steel when he heard a small knock on the door.

"Come in," he yelled.

"Daddy, I'm hungry," Shane said as he entered the room.

"Well, then get your mother to fix you some breakfast."

"Where is she?"

"She's not here?"

"No, sir."

"Well, I sure as hell don't know where she is. Just go in there and find something to eat. Cereal or cake or something that doesn't require cooking."

"Yes sir," Shane said as he ran away, excited at the prospects of making his own breakfast.

He wondered where she could be. It was certainly not like her to leave her son alone with him, especially since his suspicions had escalated. He wondered if she had left him. As he thought of that, he realized just how much he would miss her and how much he really did love her. If he could just be sure that Shane was his, he knew that they could indeed become like the happy family that was displayed in the pictures throughout their house. Just then he got an idea. Why not go to Bill's and see if she was there? But even if she were not, how could he live with her if Shane was not his son. He would be a constant and painful reminder of lost dreams and faithless deeds.

He found Shane in the kitchen making, or rather attempting to make, a balanced breakfast, something he had doubtless seen his mother do many times before.

"Shane, watch some cartoons or something until I get back. It won't be long. I'm not leaving the base."

"Yes sir. When you get back daddy, I'll have some breakfast for you."

Shane's head dropped as he heard the response to what he had just said - the slamming of the front door.

After riding past Bill's house and finding him at home alone, Stephen drove back home. Pulling up to the house, he discovered that Sandy was also just arriving.

They both slowly got out of their cars. She seemed hesitant, but he thought he sensed some of the old warmth. It was hard to tell.

"I've got some good news for you," she said as they got within a few feet of each other. Her left eye was purple and blue and swollen shut.

"Where the hell have you been?"

"I've been to see, Dr. Sills," she said. He could definitely hear some warmth in her voice, but she still kept her distance from him.

"Why? He's my doctor, not yours."

"I know, but it was the only way. I'm so ready for things to get back to the way they were. And now I truly think that they can."

"What do you mean?"

"I mean, I had Dr. Sills do a blood test for Shane and Bill and compare it to yours."

"And?"

"And, it's good news. He's going to call you himself and tell you."

They walked inside, (she never turning her back to him) to hear the phone ringing. It was Dr. Sills. It was good news.

"I'm a dad," he said for the first time with conviction, instantly losing all his previous embarrassment over Dr. Sills and Bill knowing about his suspicions. "Oh God San, I'm so sorry. Please forgive me."

They embraced. The world seemed to become silent and still. Until she heard thunder and felt her husband start with fright. He let her go and started toward the hall.

"What is it?" She said as she followed him.

As they reached the hall, she could smell gun powder and smoke and knew that it was not thunder she had heard at all.

"Oh God, Stephen, where is Shane?"

He didn't answer.

"Steve!" she screamed, though she was right behind him. "Answer me damn it!"

He flung the door open and stood there frozen in the doorway, unable to move. Stephen's body blocked most of her view, but she could see the centerpiece of the room - the hunting picture of Steve and his dad - covered with blood.

THE MEASURE OF A SIN

Sin is and does all the horrible things that we thus far have attributed to its nature. We know what is considered to be sin, but how do we know what sin is? For example, we know that the pride, faithlessness, obsession, and neglect of the father in the story, *The Wages of Sin*, was sin, but how do we know that pride, faithlessness, obsession, and parental neglect are sins. In other words, how can we know what sin is and what sin is not? Is it a purely subjective query? Is my sin only that which I deem to be sin and your sin only that which you think sin to be, or is there a more objective standard. How can we know?

The fact is, we didn't know what sin was until the law was given. God's law is the standard by which sin is judged. According to St. Paul, sin was in the world long before the law was given, however, since there was no standard, there was no responsibility. The law was given to reveal our sin to us. The law of God is the instrument of measurement by which we are all measured.

Rather than leaving us to our own subjective feelings, beliefs, or consciences, God gave to us an objective standard. The law reveals what is right, in order that we might know also what is wrong. The law of God, in its entirety, which includes but is not limited to the ten commandments, is that which is just, right, and pleasing to God. The law of God reveals to us the will of God for us.

And yet, the law was not given to make us righteous. Contrary to what many people believe, the law was not given primarily to be kept, but to be broken. In fact, the law was broken before it was given, thus, the account of Moses breaking the tablets of the law upon his return from Mt. Sinai. This was merely an outward and visible sign of what was already an inward and spiritual reality. The primary purpose of the law was the exposing and revealing of sin and not rules for righteousness.

Many people today, in error, seek to keep the external commandments of God, seeking to be justified by them. These same people have a sense of accomplishment and self-righteousness because they feel they have kept the law. This does two detrimental things. First, it reduces the law, which is the heart of God, to a simple set of religious "do's" and "don't's." Secondly, it invalidates the true purpose of the law in their lives. The truth is, the law was given not to justify, but to condemn.

If you are seeking to be justified by the law, then you are working contrary to the will of God. The sin of perversion is nowhere more visible than in the twisting of God's purpose for the law into our own. Trying to rid ourselves of sin with the law is as futile as trying to saw lumber with a yardstick. The law was not made to remove sin, but rather to reveal it.

We, each and everyone of us, can know definitively what sin is because of the revealed law of God. There is nothing left for conjecture or guess work, it is all revealed within the law. The law of God is plain, leaving nothing to question. God's law does not reveal who is guilty, but rather that all are guilty.

Finally, the law is a school master. The law was given in order to lead us to something else. There are many things that we can learn from the law including: what sin is, our sinfulness, and our inability to keep the law. We must recognize and appreciate the law's purpose and its possibilities. However, we must recognize its limits too. The law is a school master intended to lead us to . . . .

**DADDY'S ANGEL
a story**

She sat in the plush waiting room, palms sweaty and heart racing, waiting to see Dr. Allen James Coefield. The room, like the man, was both impressive and imposing. He was not only an M.D. with an extremely prosperous psychiatric practice, the head of the psychology department at the University, the host of a nationally syndicated radio talk show, author of five bestsellers, but he was also her father.

She could not recall the number of times she had sat in his waiting room waiting to see him. However, she had never had to wait very long. All she had to do was to let his receptionist know that she wished to see him, and as quickly as possible, he would materialize. Sometimes that was as much as fifty minutes, but never once had it been over fifty minutes. Each of his sessions were exactly fifty minutes long, and though he could not stop in the middle of one, he would rush out to see her as soon as his session had ended.

Today, however, she had asked his receptionist not to tell him she was there until he had seen his last patient. Of course, this meant waiting, but she didn't mind, she just wanted to be the last person to see him. If she were going to ruin his day she could at least wait until it was almost over before she did it. She feared, not so much that she might ruin his day, but that she might actually ruin his life. Besides, she could use this time to prepare what she would say to him, because she really had no idea.

Sitting there, as a seventeen-year-old, was quite a different experience from sitting there five years earlier as a twelve-year-old waiting to tell her dad that she had won first place at the all-state speech competition. She waited then, unlike now, impatiently. Then, unlike now, she was dying to tell him the news, for many reasons, but most of all because his approval meant more to her than anything in the world. After waiting for what seemed like two eternities, which was actually less than ten minutes, the patient whose session she had fought not to interrupt came out of the door with her dad right behind her.

"There's Daddy's little Angel," he said, like he always did, and beckoned her into his office. "So tell me, how did you do?" he said as he effortlessly hoisted her up onto his lap after he was seated on the leather couch to the left of his desk.

"I got third place, dad, aren't you proud?"

"I expected more."

"But daddy, they were all so good. I was competing against our state's best speakers."

"Yes, I know Angel, but you are our state's best speaker."

"You really think so, dad?" she asked with a wry little grin.

"Yes, I do," he said definitively.

"They did too," she said as she pulled the small gold medallion from her pocket.

"You little stinker," he said, and with that started to tickle her.

"I am not," she protested, "I'm Daddy's Angel."

"Daddy's proud of his little Angel too."

This visit, five years later, she sat there filling her three-hour wait with just such memories. Most of her memories were like that one - positive and affirming - but it is little wonder since she was, in fact, an angel, or, as close as you could get to being one and still remain human. For as long as she could remember, she had made him proud, and for as long as she could remember, making him proud was what she wanted to do more than anything.

Not all her memories were positive ones though. There were some that were less than perfect, some that stung just a little as she thought about them. It seemed that those were the ones that had been more recent and had begun to occur with much more frequency. She noticed a pattern, perhaps even an escalation in his expectations of her, and her disappointments of him. She wondered if she was still daddy's angel. Daddy's Angel - it's funny but he had called her that for so long that everyone else called her

Angel, even though her name was Amy.

    One of her less than perfect memories had occurred only two months back. Although she was only a junior, she had already met all the requirements for high school graduation. She had come to tell him that not only was she not the very top of her graduating class, but also that she was received by not the first university of his choice - his old alma mater, but his second choice, of which he had said, "It will only do in a pinch." The thing was, he had never been, so far as she knew, in a pinch in all of his perfect life. Then, like now, it was difficult to tell him, though it was nothing so horrible as her present news. And, then, like now, she had waited until he had finished seeing all of his patients. After which, she knocked on his door and went in.

"Dad," she said. She had not called him "daddy" in quite some time.

"Angel," he said. He had dropped the 'Daddy's' part of 'Daddy's Angel' about the same time she had dropped the 'y' from 'daddy'. "Come on in. How are you?"

"I'm okay."

"Just okay? What is it?"

"Well, I placed second in my class and I got accepted to the second university we wanted and not the first," she blurted out in record speed.

"You little stinker," he said as he laughed, "That's not going to work on me this time."

"I'm not joking, dad. I'm not being a stinker. I guess I'm not being an angel either, but I'm not teasing. I'm serious."

He could tell she was.

He said, "It's okay, Angel," but she knew that it wasn't. She had let him down. She was devastated, as she assumed he was too, and that had been nothing compared to what she waited to tell him this day.

    Sitting there, still contemplating what she would say to him. She looked down at the end table next to her chair and saw his picture on the cover of *Recovery* magazine. Why did he have to be so damn perfect? Why did everything come so easily to him? It wasn't fair. Why couldn't she have a dad like one of her many friends who never even saw their dads, much less answered to them. She considered that perhaps there was a mistake at the hospital when she was born and that she was not his daughter at all. She didn't think that was really true. But she knew one thing was true, she did not, nor did she ever feel she could, live up to his legacy.

Finally, after his last patient was long gone, she slowly walked toward the door. She knew he would be mad, that he would take vengeance, but above the beating or the punishment she would receive, was the fact, the horrible fact, that she had let him down. He had never hit her before, but if he was ever going to, this would be the time. By the time she raised her hand to knock on his door she was trembling all over. She lightly tapped on the door. He obviously did not hear her. She knocked harder. To her utter horror, he heard the second knock. She started to run away, but somehow stayed.

"Come in," his rich baritone voice boomed through the closed door.

"It's me, dad," she said as she walked through the door.

"Angel, what a nice surprise. Come in. Come in. How are you?"

"Not too good daddy," she said as her tears began to flow.

"Angel, what is it?"

Never one to beat around the bush, she said, "Daddy, I've done something awful. I have been dishonest with the university, you, and God. I am removing my name from the scholarship list and withdrawing from the fall semester. And I will accept any punishment you see fit."

"Why? What is it? What did you do?"

"I cheated on the scholarship tests," she said bravely, and then drew back awaiting his wrathful response.

"You did?" he asked, in amazement.

"I know how angry you must be, and disappointed. I've let you down. I know you wish I was not your daughter. I wish I was not. I'm so sorry."

At that, he stood and walked around the desk to where she was. "Stand up," he said.

She immediately complied, with much trepidation however. When she was standing fully erect, he raised his arm. Without even thinking, she ducked and put her arms up in a defensive position. He merely put his arm around her, pulled her toward him and hugged her long and hard.

"Don't ever say that I wish you were not my daughter, because nothing could ever be further from the truth. I love you. You are, and will always be, my angel."

"Fallen angel," she whispered.

"Perhaps, for the moment, but no less angel, and no less mine."

They both began to cry and embrace even harder. After a long while, she broke the silence.

"But I cheated. I don't deserve your love. I failed you," she said beginning to cry again.

"I love you. You are lovable and you do deserve my love, but it was never based on your deserving it, it has always been," he thought for a minute, "I love you, and there is no way I could ever stop loving you. I will always love you, and there is nothing that you could ever do to change that."

"But you laid down the law and I broke it."

"Sometimes you have to break the law to experience what is beyond it."

BEYOND THE LAW

Daddy's Angel discovered what was beyond the law only after she had broken the law. Each of us as flawed and fallible human beings have the same opportunity. Sin is a human condition - part of our very nature. God's law was given to us so that we might know what sin is and that we are sinners. However, we must realize that the purpose of the law is not exclusively to reveal to us our sinful nature, but also to lead us to the solution for that nature. The law alone is not the solution.

The law gives us a crystal clear picture of how things should be, but it does not give us the means by which to achieve those things. The law is like many sermons I hear preached these days. They tell people what they should be and do, but not how to become that person and not how to do those things.

The giving of the law was like the passing of a death sentence because our sin becomes death when judged by the law. And, the law itself becomes death when we seek to be justified by it, because we can never be. This is okay, though, because it is not the purpose of the law to save. The law was intended to make sin lethal to be sure, but it was not intended to then kill us, but to lead us to what is beyond the law.

That which is beyond the law is grace. Grace is more powerful than both sin and the law. The law brings death, but grace brings life. Sin is revealed by the law in order to further reveal to us our need for grace. When we sin, the law offers no comfort or solution. It merely states our guilt and sentence. However, this should point us to our need for mercy. Mercy is God's gift of love to us in the form of grace.

God lays down the law, we break his law, and in doing so, discover the power of his love that is greater than the law. The letter of the law kills, but the spirit of the law gives life. The letter of the law pronounces our guilt, the spirit of the law pronounces to us God's love for us in spite of that guilt. True redemption begins when we are condemned by the law, see our powerlessness to keep the law, and become open to God's gracious gift of love, which is not based on our keeping the law, but on his infinite capacity of love.

I am beginning to understand this, in part, because of what I have learned from those in my life that I love. The true love that I feel for my loved ones is not based on their behavior, in fact, it's not based on anything, it just is. Thus, is the illogical nature of love. Love is foolish and illogical because it is never based on the lovableness of the person loved, rather it just inexplicably exists.

I love my children Meleah and Micah, not because of their worthiness, thought they are very worthy of my love, but simply because I can't help but love them. You notice, of course, that I stated definitively their worthiness to be loved. Who says so? I do. And, I am the one doing the loving, therefore, my love for them makes them worthy of my love. Similarly, God's love for me, by virtue of its very existence, makes me worthy of his love. I am worthy of God's love, not because I am able to keep his rules, but because he says that I am by loving me.

I feel confident in my worthiness to be loved by God. I do not, however, feel that I have earned this worthiness, but that his love makes me worthy to be loved. This is, in great part, do to my earthly parents. Their unconditional love of me, despite my many imperfections, bad manners, ill-behavior, and my obnoxious personality, has convinced me that my heavenly parents can love me unconditionally as well. (Parents who have ears, let them hear - you are your children's first image of God.)

My parents' love for me, and my love for my children have served as an extremely vivid object lesson and metaphor for God's love for me. I am loved. God loves me. I am worthy of that love, simply because he loves me.

PHYSICIAN, HEAL THY SON
a story

He had never quite done what his father had wanted him to do. His older brother, on the other hand, had always done exactly what his father had wanted. This was no small feat because doing what Robert James Robertson wished was nearly impossible, not to mention that his wishes were really not wishes at all, but demands. As the youngest, he had been given certain latitude that his older brother had not. Jerry was seen, or rather saw himself, not as rebellious or irresponsible, but as a free-spirit. His father could count on his older brother, but he was the one that brought true joy to his father's heart. He had always felt that his father was really much more like him than he allowed himself to be. After all, how could his father be the most respected medical researcher in the field of infectious disease and the head of the world renown infectious disease research center at the University of Miami and be a free-spirit. His brother, Robert James Robertson II, saw him as a spoiled brat, but it was more complicated than that and his father knew it.

The relationship that Jerry, Robert, and Robert Jr. shared had almost always been strained. Robert Jr. was only eleven and a half months older than Jerry, causing the boys to be reared, to behave, and to be perceived as twins. From the beginning, a fierce competition existed between the two boys. Although the competition existed between the two boys, it always centered around pleasing their father. So it was, that their aunt Dorene referred to them as Esau and Jacob, and in a self-fulfilling prophecy, Jerry reached for and grabbed the heel of Robert Jr. by skipping an entire year at the University of Miami graduated at the same time as his older brother. In fact, Jerry actually walked down the isle to the tune of *Pomp and Circumstance* before Robert Jr. because "J" comes before "R".

After walking down the graduating isle together, the two Robertson boys went in separate directions. Not entirely separate directions – they both went to medical school - just different ones and for different reasons. Jerry went to medical school in order to become a pediatrician.

Specializing in pediatrics meant that he would be a physician like his father but not in the exact same profession. This seemed to Jerry to be the perfect tightrope walk on the fine line between honoring his dad and honoring his own commitment to autonomy. Of course, Robert Jr. went not only into the same field as his father, but also into the exact same profession. This crossroads in their lives and the manner in which each responded, best defined their relationship with their father.

The summer after their college graduation, there were many discussions about the two boy's futures in medicine.

"Have you heard anything about my application for admissions, dad?" Robert Jr. asked.

"No, son, why would I?"

"Well, contrary to what you say, I know that even your esteemed colleagues at the University have been known to gossip now and then."

"Have you heard from any of the other universities that you applied to yet?"

"No, sir."

"See, I told you it was still far too early."

"It's not that. It's that I didn't apply to any except Miami. I want to work with you, dad and one day carry on your work."

"I think I'm going to be sick," Jerry piped in.

"Shut up," Robert Jr. retorted.

"Son," Robert Sr. said, addressing Robert Jr., "I am proud that you want to work with me."

At this Robert Jr. beamed.

"However," his dad continued, "It was foolish to apply to only one school."

"As far as I am concerned, there is only one school," Robert Jr. said, milking it for everything that it was worth.

"What you really mean is that if you have any hope of getting into medical school with your test scores it will have to be the one that dad practically runs single-handedly," Jerry said with a very cold smile.

"You little bastard, you know that's not true. That's not true is it, dad?"

"No, son, it's not entirely true."

"What do you mean, 'not entirely true'?"

"I mean it is pretty damned convenient and safe that I am on staff at the one school you applied to."

"On staff?" Jerry said, "Dad you're a living legend."

"I don't care what you say, I want to work with dad and that's the only reason that I applied in the first place so why apply any place else? Miami may be the only place that I applied, but you didn't apply here at all did you?"

"No, I didn't," Jerry said with no hesitation.

Robert Sr. raised an eyebrow and said, "I was not aware that you didn't even apply here at home. Why not?"

"Simple," Jerry said looking at Robert Jr. "I want to make it on my own."

"I have no doubt that you will, son," his dad said. "Where is it that you want to go?

"The University of Florida."

"I see. And what kind of scholarship did they offer you?"

"None at all. That's what I wanted to talk to you about. Can I have the cash?"

"If you're accepted," his dad said.

"If I'm accepted?" Jerry asked in mock disbelief

"What about the other schools that did offer you scholarships?"

"I, like my older brother, it pains me to say, only applied to one school as well."

"See," Robert Jr. shouted, "I knew it. I knew you were trying to force dad's hand too."

"So you were trying to force dad's hand to get you in to Miami Med?"

"That's not what I meant."

"Well what did you mean, Bobby?" Jerry continued, calling him by a nick-name he hated, "Because it's what you said. So if it's not, why'd you say it?"

"I'm not going to argue with you," Robert Jr. said, as he always did when he knew that he could not win, which was nearly every time with Jerry. "You should be a lawyer not a doctor, you slick little bastard."

"Okay, that's enough boys," Robert Sr. said, and raised his hand slightly, bringing silence almost immediately. "Now let me just get this straight, so I will know." He turned to Jerry. "You actually got a scholarship right here in Miami, but did not even apply here, but instead you applied at Gainesville where you were not offered any scholarship at all?"

"That's pretty much it," Jerry said.

"And you," Robert Sr. said to Robert Jr. "You were offered a scholarship in Maine and did not even apply there, but applied right here in Miami where you were offered no scholarship and where you would be lucky to get in?"

"That's not exactly it, but . . ."

"Robert Sr. raised his eyebrows sharply.

"Yes, sir," Robert Jr. conceded.

"Very well," Robert Sr. said and with that it was settled and nothing else was ever said about it, in front of him anyway.

The following fall Jerry moved to Gainesville, Florida and entered medical school and made many incredible discoveries. He discovered, for instance, that he could spend very little time studying and still do relatively well in all of his classes, all but one that is. He also discovered a whole new world. Like a man recently freed from incarceration, his new found liberty was overwhelming. He discovered, much to his utter amazement, just how great an effect his competition with his brother had had on him - he had drives, desires, and interest that he never allowed himself to have before. Among his most powerful discoveries were women and drugs. Both of them, he found, were much more intense than medical school. He was however, the son of a doctor and a future doctor himself, therefore, he was extremely careful with both.

The most life-altering discovery he made, however, came about quite by accident. In filling out one of his registration forms, he inadvertently put the number of the credit card his dad had given him for emergencies, thus charging his tuition and books to his dad's card. This not only gave him nearly a thousand extra dollars that month, but also went totally unnoticed by his dad's secretary - the one that paid the bills. In a matter of weeks, Jerry had escalated to the point of charging the entirety of his month's expenses to his dad's Visa Gold card and spending the twenty-five hundred dollars that was transferred into his account the beginning of each month on whatever pleased him most at the time, which always included women, booze, and drugs. Within three months he had stopped attending his classes altogether.

It was at the end of his second semester, or what would have been his second semester, that his father's secretary and his father made a discovery of their own. The credit card was canceled and the twenty-five-hundred dollar a month account to account transfer stopped. When he thought of calling his dad, which he knew that he would never do under the circumstances, it reminded him of just how long it had been since he had spoken with him. The last time they had spoken was in November, Jerry's one trip home the entire school year. As he thought about what he would do, he couldn't help but wonder how Robert Jr. was doing - he was surely not the smartest student at Miami, but Jerry bet he was the most determined.

As he could not file for unemployment because he had never been employed, something that he honestly did not know when he went to file for it, Jerry began to consider his employment options. He didn't have many. Of the two jobs he was offered, changing the diapers of and bathing elderly people whom nobody cared for was the best. It was at this time, out of the blue, like tragedy always does, that his world, or what little remained of it, fell a part. His blood test at the time of his interview came back with a "little problem," the nurse said. Jerry wondered what it could be because he hadn't had money for drugs in months. However, when the doctor passed the sentence, it carried much more weight than a prognosis. Jerry wished it would have been a little thing like getting caught with cocaine in his blood. Instead, it was a death sentence. The doctor had said HIV, but all that Jerry heard was DEATH. On his own, in less than a year, Jerry was homeless, penniless, and hopeless. He would have laughed, he wanted to laugh at his folly, but he could not. He tried, but he could not.

For several weeks, depressed out of his mind, Jerry laid in a homeless shelter waiting for the death train to arrive. Having to wait seemed so cruel now that he knew it was coming. Of all trains, this one should never be late, but it was. While waiting to catch his final train, he heard two of the other homeless men, both of which he shared HIV as well as homelessness with, saying that there was a new HIV research project at the University of Miami looking for guinea pigs for new experimental HIV drugs. Jerry instantly knew what he must do. And he did it.

After hitchhiking back down to Miami, he went to the building where his dad's offices were, and no doubt the new project was. From a phone booth on the corner he called his dad's secretary to feel out the situation. He knew it would not be a pretty sight, but he wanted to know just how bad it would be. Standing there in front of the building he had entered and exited so many times before, back when times were better, he suddenly became very self conscious of his appearance. His clothes were dirty, wrinkled, and torn and his hair was tangled and matted. When Linda heard his voice her first question was, "where are you?" She wanted to know because his dad had been looking for him everywhere. In fact, he had hired a private investigator to track him down. He learned that his dad knew everything already and still wanted to talk to him - no doubt to tell him how disgusted he was with him. He told her his location anyway because he needed to be told how disgusting he was just then. He asked her where his dad was and she told him to please hold on for a moment. When she came back to the line she was acting very strangely. He could not get a straight answer from her no matter what he did. Suddenly it occurred to him that she may have called the police, after all he had stolen a great deal of his dad's money.

He slammed the phone down and began to run when from the corner of his eye he could see his dad running toward him, something he had never seen before in his whole life. He started to run from him, then he started to just cover his head with his arms in a defensive position and take the beating he deserved, and then he decided to stand up to him like the man he had raised him to be.

"Before you say anything, dad," he said when his dad was within hearing distance, "I want to say that I know what I did was wrong, and I alone am to blame. I know I really don't deserve to be your son, but could I at least be your patient?"

The second he finished what he had to say, his father reached him, sweating and out of breath, but rather than stopping short of where he was, his dad ran all the way up to him and threw his arms around him and they embraced for a long time. For them the world stood still, even thought the automobile and pedestrian traffic continued to move past them on the busy Miami street. As they continued to embrace, Jerry could hear the sound of the death train's whistle growing more and more faint until he could no longer hear it at all and Robert Sr.'s vision of his son in a cheap coffin in a shabby old funeral home surrounded by strangers faded to black.

"Son, I love you. You can be my patient, but you will always be, first and foremost, my beloved son, who makes my heart dance. Now, come on, let's go home. I've prepared your old room with all the necessary equipment and an around-the-clock staff."

"Why do all this, I'm going to be dead soon?" Jerry asked.

"No, son, you were dead to me, but now you're alive again. Risen from the dead."

Later that evening, Robert Jr. kept the promise he had made not to stay in the house if Jerry was there. As he was loading the last of his things into his car, his dad came outside to talk with him.

"I wish you wouldn't do this son."

"I wish *you* wouldn't do this. I damn sure know that you wouldn't do it for me. He wasted your money on drugs and whores and now he's getting what he deserves and you still love him. He's being punished for what he's done."

"He certainly is, son, so we don't have to do it. What we have to do is to love him and thank God above that the prodigal has come home."

WHEN SIN IS GRACE

Like the daughter in *Daddy's Angel* or the son in *Physician, Heal Thy Son*, with full knowledge of what God wanted from me, I did that which God told me not to, in order to really understand God's grace. God laid down the law, I broke his law, and came running back to him and found what was beyond the law - his grace.

This is the most perplexing and paradoxical thing about the whole issue - it took sinning for me to experience grace. In fact, every time you and I have an occasion of sin, we have, at the exact same moment, an occasion of grace. For, as St. Paul said, *"But where sinned increased, grace increased all the more."*

Herein lies the purpose of the law. *"The law was added so that the trespass might increase, but where sin increased, grace increased all the more."* When is sin grace? Sin is grace when we see that our God loves us, though we reject him and break his laws. The law was given to show us that we can't keep the law and to simultaneously show us our need for God's, nearly irresistible grace.

The damnedable thing of it is that those that keep the law, or think they do, never truly experience what is more powerful than the law - grace. Paradoxically, we come to know the nature of God the most in times when we have obeyed him the least. In case you are not familiar with love or have forgotten what it really is - this is it at its foolish and illogical best. Love is not love until it is given to the unlovable, or at least to the less than lovable.

When is sin grace? When we receive the revelation that we can't help who we are - sinners, and yet realize that God loves us anyway. An occasion of sin is an occasion for grace because it is our sin that shows us our need for grace. God did not give us laws for the sole purpose of condemnation, but that through the condemnation of the law, we would reach out for what is our only hope - not more laws, but grace. Where sin abounds, grace abounds all the more! Historically, those that have enjoyed the most intimacy with God are those who have sinned, recognized their sin, admitted their sin to God, and been willing to receive his grace.

A FEW BIBLICAL EXAMPLES

In the beginning God gave his children one primary rule, "Don't eat the fruit of the tree of the knowledge of good and evil." However, those children were much like you and I and ate of the tree anyway. Do you think God was surprised? If he was, he didn't show it. What he did was to make a sacrifice to cover their shame and guilt and make a promise that one day his grace would completely remove their guilt and shame and restore to them what their sin had forfeited. That was grace.

A parallel can be drawn between the sins of Israel's first two kings -Saul and David. Both men abused their powerful positions for sinful purposes. Saul disobeyed God's command to destroy all of the Amalekites, by sparing their king as a personal trophy and their herds for free sacrifices (catch the contradiction). David, on the other hand, stole the wife of one of his most faithful soldiers and then had him killed. The sins of the two kings have direct parallels. The responses of the two kings, however, do not. Saul responded attempting to justify his sin. When this failed he began making excuses. David, on the other hand, responded by openly admitting his sin and begging for God's mercy. Saul reaped the wages of his sin - death. David discovered the true nature of God and became a merciful man and an intimate of God.

David's prayer for forgiveness is one of the most beautiful examples of how sin can become grace. Notice that each phrase is a step away from sin and a step toward grace.

> *Have mercy on me, O God, according to your unfailing love; according to your great compassion blot out my transgressions.*
> *Wash away all of my iniquity and cleanse me from my sin.*
> *For I know my transgressions, and my sin is always before me.*
> *Against you, you only, have I sinned and done what is evil in your sight, so that you are proved right when you speak and justified when you judge.*
> *Surely I was sinful at birth, sinful from the time my mother conceived me.*
> *Surely you desire truth in the inner parts; you teach me wisdom in the inmost place.*
> *Cleanse me with hyssop, and I will be clean; wash me, and I will be whiter than snow.*
> *Let me hear joy and gladness; let the bones that you have crushed rejoice.*
> *Hide your face from my sins and blot out my all my iniquity.*
> *Create in me a pure heart, O God, and renew a steadfast spirit within me.*
> *Do not cast me from your presence or take your Holy Spirit from me.*
> *Restore unto me the joy of your salvation and grant to me a willing spirit, to sustain me.*
> *Then I will teach transgressors your ways, and sinners will turn back to you.*
> *Save me from blood guilt, O God, the God who saves me, and my tongue will sing of your righteousness.*
> *O Lord, open my lips, and my mouth will declare your praise.*
> *You do not delight in sacrifice, or I would bring it; you do not take pleasure in burnt offerings.*
> *The sacrifices of God are a broken spirit; a broken and contrite heart, O God you will not despise.*
> *In your good pleasure make Zion prosper; build up the walls of Jerusalem.*
> *Then there will be righteous sacrifices, whole burnt offerings to delight you; then bulls will be offered on your altar.* Ps. 51

There is , I believe, another parallel, this time between two of Jesus' disciples. And, again, the parallel exists between their sins and not between their responses. The first disciple is Judas, who, after stealing from Jesus Christ Ministries Inc. for a number of years, finally sold

Jesus for the price of a slave with the money set aside for purchasing Passover lambs. This, in my opinion, qualifies as a breaking of the law. He, like Saul, did not repent, but rather returned the money and, remembering what the wages of sin were, attempted to pay for his sin with his life. The other disciple was Peter, who, when asked if he knew the Lord said, "Hell no, I don't know him. Are you out of your freakin' mind?" And then, he heard the three crows. Later, he responded to Jesus' offer of love and mercy with acceptance and service. And, that service, was to deliver the inaugural message of Jesus' first church.

Mary Magdalene was another poor soul that discovered an occasion of grace hidden inside her occasion of sin. After hookin' for quite some time, she was asked to pay the price for her sin and the sin of her latest John too, apparently, because he wasn't there. However, His Grace, Prince Jesus, stepped in and found grace for her even within the law of Moses, and she responded with acceptance, service, and gratitude. Many people actually believe that she fell in love with His Grace. I do. Because I did.

St. Paul, who has provided many of the original thoughts for this book, discovered God's grace in a most powerful and profound way, precisely because he didn't start out as a saint. St. Paul is the saint who described himself as, "Chief among sinners." He murdered the first people to claim that they had received grace from God through Jesus, and in doing so, found that same grace for himself. Prior to his experience with grace, Paul had been an expert in justification through the law. After having the true nature of his own sin revealed to him, Paul became the chief advocate for humanity's need for grace, experiencing first hand the inability of the law to redeem him.

Perhaps the greatest picture of this whole concept comes in the form of a story, from the master storyteller of all time. It is a story with all the great stuff stories are made of - sibling rivalry, rebellion, illicit sex, drink 'til you puke parties, the loss of family, fortune, and faith, and lots of sin, sin, sin. However, in the midst of all of this, there is grace, too. It is the greatest story ever told of how sin can become grace. It is the story that my story, *Physician, Heal Thy Son* was loosely based on - *The Parable of the Prodigal Son*.

THE PRODIGAL SON

"*There was a man who had two sons,*" is how the story begins. And, with this beginning, Jesus sets the stage of our minds with characters just like us. We are not given very much detail about these three characters. In fact, we are given just enough information to know that they are just like us. These are everyday men, and who better to tell us about ourselves.

A message lies within Jesus' choice of only three characters for his story. Why just three? If the choice of characters is the most crucial part of a story, then why just three so nondescript characters as these? Perhaps Jesus chose only three in order to force us to chose one of the three with which to identify. Jesus' stories are never cluttered with filler characters that distract us from identifying with the main ones. And maybe, he tells us nothing about who they are so that we might know everything about them. For, they are us.

Immediately after these characters have been placed inside our heads, the younger son comes to his father with a strange request, "*Father, give me my share of the estate.*" With this request the son says far more than most of us probably realize. He says, in essence, "*I can no longer wait around here until you die, so give me what is coming to me now.*" Therefore, within the younger son's request was the implied desire, "*I wish you were dead.*"

As strange as the younger son's request was, the response of the father was all the more bizarre. Surprisingly, the father, divided up the property between his two sons. Fully aware of the implications of his son's request, the father grants him his wish. This is unprecedented. How could a father do such a thing for a son who has grown weary of waiting for him to die? Could the father truly be a lunatic, or could he be showing true love?

Not long after his father was foolish enough to give him his half of the inheritance, the younger son left home.

He did not, however, just move across the street, or even across town, but to another country altogether. The younger son's leaving was not merely the fulfillment of his wish to see more of the world now that he possessed the funds to do so. Rather, it was a rejection of his home, his father, his community, and his God. He left the lifestyle, traditions, beliefs, and faith. The prodigal's leaving and the distance he traveled to flee home was nothing short of a radical rejection of his dad, his God, and their ways.

The younger son's search for identity and significance led him to spend all of his inheritance on substance abuse, whores, and the like. His money was spent on that which most contradicted the life he had known at home - his dad's life, once his life, but no longer. He refused himself nothing that he desired, like Solomon before him. And, like Solomon, he too found nothing of comfort. However, not even the vanity and futility of his indulgence caused him to turn towards home.

Finally, after all was spent and a severe famine came upon the land, he sought employment. However, the spoiled rich kid had no useful skills, in addition to being a foreigner. It was at this point, completely alone and completely empty, that he came to his senses. Realizing what he had at home, he decides to return to his dad and ask to be one of his well cared for slaves. He turns toward home.

Somehow, his father get's wind of his coming, and as he approaches, his father runs out to meet him. This is very strange behavior from a rejected father whose son had wished him dead. Nevertheless, the boy approaches his father and quickly makes his confession, "Father, I have sinned against heaven and against you. I am no longer worthy to be called your son; make me like one of your hired servants."

The father, rather than beating or berating the boy, or even telling him, "I told you so," is so over joyed to see him that he accepts the boy back in full sonship, no questions asked. The father seems so happy to have his son back that he doesn't care about the circumstances it took to force him back home. The father makes no attempt to teach the boy a lesson, to rebuke him, lay down the law again, or anything at all, but to accept him.

The son, expecting to be made a slave, is restored to full sonship with a new inheritance to squander away. His dad, the one that laid down the law in the first place, seems almost oblivious to the severity with which the son broke it. The father convinces the son that having him back home is really all that matters. It is at this point that his dad shows him how to really throw a party.

Good story. But, it's not over yet. The older son, the one who received his inheritance but stayed home, comes back from work that evening and hears the celebration. "What the hell is going on here?" he asks one of the slaves. Or, the Hebrew equivalent "Haven't you heard, " the slave responds, "your little brother is home again and the old man is so happy to see him that he threw this party." This news made the older son so angry that he refused to even go in the house.

When the father heard that the older brother was out in the field sulking, he went out to him. "Why, after all he's done to you, do you welcome him back like some kind of war hero? He, if anything, is more of a whore than a hero." The father tells the son that he can't help himself, that his boy was dead and is now alive again. To this the older son replies that he had been there all this time and he had never received such a party. To which the dad said that he could have and that the fact that he hadn't had was his own fault.

This powerful story is, in my opinion, the best story about grace that has ever been told. It is actually three stories. First, it is the story of a boy who had to get lost before he could truly be found. Secondly, it is a story about a boy who was an heir, but lived like a slave. Finally, and most importantly, it is the story of a dad, who loves unconditionally, who lays down the law, and who when his law has been broken, gives grace.

One brother gets lost and looses it all and is found. The other brother remains found and winds up lost. One brother lives outwardly by the rules, but inwardly his heart is not truly his fathers. The other brother breaks the outward rules, but has a heart the was always his fathers. The younger brother turned his occasion of sin into an occasion of grace, while the other brother turned his occasion of grace into sin.

More importantly than the two brothers that are so much like us, is the father who is so unlike us. He is a father who is patient, kind, wise, and most of all, loving. His heart beats with his children. He loves them so much, in fact, that he lets them go. He gives rules they can break, so he can give them grace when they do. He gives to each of them opportunities for sin, and simultaneously opportunities for grace too. His is unconditional love.

THE SEVEN STEPS FROM SIN TO GRACE

Is it possible for you and I to experience an occasion of grace every time we sin? Can we consistently turn our failures in the flesh into victories of the spirit? I believe that this is not only possible, but it is actually what God intends to happen. Just as with every problem there is also an opportunity for a solution, with every sin there is also an opportunity for grace.

That there is grace in the midst of our sin, I have no doubt. Whether or not you and I will experience that grace on a continual basis remains to be seen. However, it doesn't have to be based on blind luck. Certain spiritual principles can guide us to grace consistently. If I understand the purpose of the Bible at all, it is as a book filled with just such principles.

I have discovered seven principles of turning sin into grace in the biblical stories I have examined where this occurrence took place. I believe these principles to be the keys to unlocking the doors of grace to us on an ongoing basis. To assist you with memorizing them, I have used words that begin with the letter 'r'. However, these are principles, not rules, and therefore, can be expressed in many different ways.

REALIZATION

The first thing you and I must do, following the pattern of King David and the prodigal son, is to realize what we have done. *"Remember the height from which you have fallen! Repent and do the things you did at first,"* is what Jesus told the church of Ephesus. Many people never stop to consider what they have done or how far astray they have gone, and therefore, never realize the separation that has resulted from their sin. The first step, without which no other steps can be taken, is the recognition of sin for what it is and for what it has done.

In Jesus' story, the prodigal is said to have come to his senses. For the prodigal, realization came as the result of his circumstances. When he had lost it all and found himself completely alone, he finally realized what he had done and where he was. Often, quite often in fact, it takes crisis or severe loss for you and I to come to our senses - to realize how far we have fallen. Circumstances are not always a sign, and as signs go, they are often unreliable. However, we must listen to our lives for any and every message that it might contain.

Thankfully, circumstance are not God's only source of communication to us. Among the many other ways in which God communicates to us, one is through other people. This was King David's experience. David, either unable or unwilling to hear God through his heart or his circumstances, was confronted by God's spokesperson, the prophet, Nathan. When David would hear no other message, God sent him another person to speak to him. Nathan became to David the voice of God.

I wonder how often you and I are actually hearing the voice of God when we think we are just hearing our spouse, child, parent, friend, or spiritual leader. People are not our sole source of hearing from God, but they are a primary one that we would do well to listen to carefully that we might not just hear, but also perceive. David's willingness to hear God through human instrumentality led him to the realization required to began the journey away from sin and into grace.

Coming to our senses is vital because most of the sin and evil that we commit is because of inhumanity and unconsciousness. To be less than fully conscious is to be unaware and unfeeling, and capable of things that conscious people are not capable of. Often, through addiction, substance abuse, and denial we have lost our senses and our sensitivity to God and others and therefore, must have a reawakening. We must have our numbness removed and our sensitivity returned in order to realize our dilemma.

RETURN

The second step away from sin and towards grace is just that - a step toward grace. After we have come to our senses and realized what we have done and where we are, we must then begin the process of returning. It is just that simple. Turn around and head back toward grace.

When the prodigal son finally came to his senses, his first thought was to return to his father's house. He decided to return, though unaware of the grace that awaited him - he just knew that he must return. The moment we realize what we have done we must take that first step back toward home. However, we often, like Adam and Eve, are tempted to run further away from home rather than back toward it.

David didn't have a physical journey to accompany his spiritual one like the prodigal did. He did, however, have a spiritual journey. David's spiritual journey back to God began the moment he realized what he had done. It was at that moment, with no hesitation, that David fell on his face before God and in doing so began the long walk home.

The simple truth is that often the one difference between those who find grace and those who do not is the willingness to return. When everything in us says to run and hide, we must find the wisdom to run back toward God. Wether it is the prodigal son taking that first step on his long journey home or King David falling prostrate before God, the prophet, his friends, and subjects, we must return to God once we realize how far away from him we are.

RECOGNITION

Once we realize our condition and begin our return, we must recognize our sin. So often, even after being confronted with or by our sin, we still fail to truly acknowledge it. Somehow, we continue our denial, numbness, or unconsciousness, just to a lesser degree.

However, the third step away from sin and toward grace is the full acknowledgment of our sin. Rather than claiming to be innocent, ignorant, or inventing excuses, we must fully recognize our sin.

David, when asking for God's forgiveness for his sin, began by saying, *"I acknowledge my sin and my transgressions are ever before me."* David, unlike Saul before him, made no attempt at deception and offered no excuses. He quickly admitted his sin and took full responsibility for it.

When the prodigal son returned to his father he quickly recognized his actions as sinful and never once offered an excuse. We must do the same. We must know our sin - study it even. We should know how it begins, how it grows, and how it manifests. To fully acknowledge it is to know it fully. To fully know it, is our only hope of not repeating it.

Seeking to justify our sin when we are confronted with it, is the costly mistake that Adam, Eve, Saul, and countless others have made. David and the prodigal son could have easily made excuses, but they realized the futility of such action. Rather than assigning blame or guilt, we must acknowledge that we have sinned. For, if we do not, we miss the grace that results from such acknowledgment.

REPENTANCE

The fourth step away from sin and toward grace is confession. Once we realize our predicament, return to God, recognize our sin, we must then confess and repent of our sin. The power of confession can scarcely be overestimated. Confession is good for the soul - it is good for the body and spirit, too. Confessing our sin openly and honestly to God and trusted others drives out of the dark recesses of our minds the creatures of shame and guilt and forces them into the light of God's love where they are visible and more easily dealt with.

As long as we keep our guilt, fear, and shame locked inside of us, it grows to monstrous proportions. Confession, however, exposes these things and they shrink to a manageable size in the process. The power of guilt, fear, and shame is their secrecy. These things feed on darkness and denial.

David said, *"For I know my transgressions and my sin is always before me. Against you, you only, have I sinned and done what is evil in your sight."* The prodigal said, *"Father, I have sinned against heaven and against you."*

Certainly God is aware of our sin. In fact, he probably knew about it before we did it. However, he so understands our need for confession that he makes it a prerequisite for our reception of his grace. *"If we will confess our sins, he is faithful and just to forgive us."* However, we must remember the other verse in that passage that warns, *"But if we say we have no sin, we make him a liar and his truth is not in us."* Many of us miss our occasion of grace because we are unwilling to confess our sin.

"Confession is made unto salvation," is the way one writer puts it. And, I can think of no better way to express the release that honest confession brings. We are set free, delivered, and saved when we exorcize our souls of the demons that dwell there. Confession brings humility, discomfort, and embarrassment to be sure; however, it is nothing compared to the joy of salvation that follows.

REVELATION

The fifth step away from sin and toward grace is a revelation of what our sin has done. We must have the true nature of our sin revealed to us and then we must reveal it to God and others. The wages of sin are death. Sin is costly. The way of a transgressor is hard. We must realize what the penalty of our sin is and confess that to God.

Looking at the consequences of our sin will instruct us, humble us, enlighten us about other areas to be addressed, and make us realize the incredible power of God's grace.

The prodigal's revelation was revealed in his confession to his father, "*I am no longer worthy to be your son - make me as one of your servants.*" The son realized that his sin - the squandering of his inheritance and the rejection of his dad and his God - disqualified him from being a son. He realized that being a son entitled him to rights and privileges of which he had proven himself unworthy.

David's confession was similar. He said to God in his prayer that turned sin into grace, "*You are proved right when you speak and justified when you judge.*" David's prayer revealed that he had already received a revelation about the nature and consequences of his sin.

Very often, we must recognize the full extent of the consequences of our sin in order to fully deal with them. We must examine the ways in which we are reaping what we have sown. We must see how far from home our sins have caused us to journey. In doing these things we begin to understand the profound impact of grace in our lives.

RECEPTION

The next step away from sin and towards grace is reception. This step involves receiving God's grace and is far more difficult than most people realize. Once we have seen our sin for what it is and confessed it openly and honestly to God, we must then receive God's grace. However, truly seeing our sin is disturbing to us and often makes us feel unworthy to receive God's grace.

When the prodigal son's father said to him that he would restore him to full sonship he could have easily refused. He said that he was unworthy and indeed he was. And, that's just it. We must receive God's grace not because we have become worthy of it, but in spite of our unworthiness. Secretly, many of us try to deal with our sinful behavior before we take it to God; and therefore, feel as if we have earned the grace we are receiving. The reason that this step is so difficult is because it is with the full knowledge of our unworthiness to receive grace that we must be willing to receive it.

Peter received the forgiveness and grace that Jesus offered to him, though it was extremely difficult to do. It would appear that Judas did not receive that same grace from Jesus in this life (I can't say for sure; he may have). If he did not, it was because of the enormous guilt he felt because of his sin and consequently the extreme discomfort involved in receiving grace under the circumstances.

As the father's servants placed the ring of covenant on his son's finger, the robe of righteousness on his back, and the new sandals on his feet, I imagine that the prodigal son felt more uncomfortable at that moment than he ever had in his entire life. Grace is disturbing. It is disconcerting and extremely uncomfortable to receive. However, it should be received in this manner each and every time.

RESPONSE

I conclude that the final step away from sin and into grace is to respond to God's grace. In addition to receiving God's grace, which we did in the previous step, we need to go a step further and respond to God's grace. Receiving God's grace is our willingness to accept it, while responding to God's grace is doing something with it once we have received it.

While it is true that we cannot do something in order to receive grace, we must do something once we have received it. Grace is a gift, and as a gift, cannot be purchased or earned. However, as a gift, grace must be acted upon once it has been given. Receiving grace from God is not an end in itself, but is instead the means to a new lifestyle, more intimate relationships, the power to overcome, and to help others.

The response of the prodigal son was to again accept the rules of his father's house. David's response to God's grace, in addition to becoming an extremely merciful king, was seen in his prayer, *"Then I will teach transgressors your ways, and sinners will turn back to you."* And, as far as we know, neither David nor the prodigal son ever repeated their sin again.

Receiving God's grace is like receiving a gift. Responding to God's grace is how we say thank-you to God for that gift and how we use this most precious gift that we have received.

THE NATURE OF GRACE

Though I found defining sin difficult, it was quite simple compared to defining grace. Grace is even more allusive and mystical than sin. Grace is unpredictable, showing up in the strangest places and on the oddest faces. Grace is like a pleasant surprise that you least expected, but had you wished for something, it couldn't have been more perfect than the gift of grace you were given. Furthermore, you don't really know where it came from or how it got there, but you have your suspicions. Grace, is alas, a mystery to me. Big surprise, right?

Of all Christian beliefs, grace is the most important. In fact, Christianity is, in summary form, "The Gospel of God's Grace." The concept of grace is a purely and uniquely Christian concept. No other religion or discipline has at its very core the idea of grace. Other religions seek to do things to earn salvation, whereas Christianity asserts that salvation comes exclusively through grace, which is received by faith - not works, wisdom, intellect, or logic.

Many words have been employed to attempt to define what grace is. The primary one is love. Unconditional love is a grace and grace is the result of love. Love is warmth, affection, desire, kindness, and goodwill towards another person. However, the recipient is nearly irrelevant to the equation. The recipient of love may, in fact, be undeserving or unlovable, but love is nonetheless present. In this sense, love is a grace and grace involves love. Love is foolish by virtue of its being so illogical. In the same manner, grace is not given when it is deserved, but rather when it is needed. If grace were given when it was deserved it wouldn't be needed. Love and grace are both given apart from reason and justification. Once we realize this, we begin to touch on the true nature of grace.

Another word that is equated with grace is exchange. Grace is the exchange of two opposing things. God's grace is revealed in the exchange of Christ's life for ours. He didn't deserve to die and we don't deserve to live, and yet there was an exchange - life for life. However, one life was just and one life was unjust. The exchange is not fair or equatable. Jesus removed his robe of righteousness and we our robe of defilement and, the two were exchanged. Such is grace. Grace exchanges good for bad, pure for impure, right for wrong, and innocence for guilt.

Grace also involves the concept of favor. When we receive favor from someone, we are receiving grace. Grace is favor in any situation or with any person. In particular, grace is favor in situations and with people when it is not deserved. "The Precious Unmerited Favor of God," as the Dottie Rambo song says is grace. Grace occurs when we are granted favor by God, when to do so, he must violate his own laws. However, he created those laws in order that he might violate them with his grace. In this respect, then, it is not a violation, but merely a part of the most wonderful plan ever conceived.

The concept of mercy is also employed when trying to define grace. Mercy occurs when we are given what we need and not what we deserve. When we are found guilty, sentenced, and then our sentence is overturned, our execution is stayed, and our pardon is granted. Grace is mercy in action. Mercy is love in action. Grace is a full pardon. It is absolution. Grace is a wronged party choosing not to retaliate. Grace is when love blinds God to our shortcomings. God is not blind, but in his love he chooses not to see our forgiven failures. If love is blind, then grace is a choice to love in order to be blinded to the utter unlovableness of the one being loved.

Grace is a gift. Gifts are graces. It is like tearing off the bow and ripping into the wrapping paper to discover what we needed most in this world - a gift that is essential to our inner well being as air is to our physical well being. Gifts are not earned, worked for, or received at our discretion, and in those ways, they are like grace. Grace is an unexpected gift that is just the right size, color, and style of the thing we didn't just want, but we really, really needed. Grace is a gift and unable to be attained. It is what we don't deserve, like when we've been naughty and not nice, but we get it anyway. Grace is a gift.

Grace is forgiveness. When we have sinned and God forgives us, we have received grace. When we owe a debt that we cannot pay and it is paid for us, we have received grace. Wronging someone and having them not hold it against us is a grace. Hurting someone and having them respond in love rather than retaliation is forgiveness and, as such, is grace.

Finally, grace is a sacrament. The word sacrament means mystery. A sacrament is a time, place, person, or thing that mysteriously reveals God to us. When God is mysteriously involved in or through someone or thing it is a grace. Sacraments involve God's mysterious presence, which is itself a grace. God is at times experienced in or through a friend, lover, parent, child, and in each of those times it is a grace. Grace occurs the moment God comes on the scene. A sacrament is anywhere that God is mysteriously and wonderfully revealed and that is grace.

Grace is any place, thing, person, or event that brings us into contact and relationship with God. Where God is, there is grace, and grace is also the vehicle through which God comes to us. Anything that expresses God's love, care, and concern for us is a grace. Any time we pause to consider God or to thank God for something in our lives, it is grace.

THE PURPOSE OF GRACE

What then is the purpose of grace? Why is this powerful force in existence? Grace exists for several reasons, none of which would be possible without grace. All of the things that grace is and does can be summed up in one word - love. Grace is love in action. Grace is a conduit for love. Therefore, the purpose of grace is to bring us to love.

The first purpose of grace is to save us. As in the parable Jesus told about the Samaritan traveler, often times the most urgent thing for grace to do is to rescue us. Grace rescues us from ourselves, our enemies, circumstances, and at times, even from the very hand of evil. Salvation is the grace-filled process by which God spares us from death and destruction and restores to us all that we have lost and all that has been taken from us. The purpose of grace is to save.

Another purpose of grace is to release us. Each of us owe debts we cannot repay and we are imprisoned by them. We have stolen, abused, and wronged so many people that we cannot repay. We have wronged our creator and sustainer. We have rebelled against him and disobeyed his commandments to us, and we are unable to repay him. We are unable to make things right, and we are, therefore, imprisoned in guilt, pain, and darkness. God's grace is that which releases us from the prison we are in. Grace pays the price of our release from darkness into light.

Grace exists also to restore to us that which we have lost. In the case of the story of the good Samaritan the traveler has lost his way, his money, his ability to travel, and was on the verge of losing his life. The Samaritan restored to the traveler all of the things he had lost. In doing so, the Samaritan was an example of what God's grace is like. When we have been robbed, beaten, and left for dead on the side of the road, it is God's grace that comes along and lifts us out of the ditch, bandages our wounds, and carries us the rest of the way.

Another purpose of grace is to bring to our attention and call to our remembrance God's love. In the midst of an unjust world where we are cheated, mistreated, used, and abused, grace breaks through to make sure that we don't forget that in the midst of it all, God still loves us. Grace, more than any other force, demonstrates God's incredible love for us, because it usually comes when we need it most and deserve it least.

Finally, and most importantly, grace has as its goal moving us closer to God. Grace is in essence God's passionate desire for us expressed and demonstrated. God wants us, and giving us grace is her primary way of wooing us. The reason grace saves us, or releases us, or restores us, is so, that through it all, God can be with us. Grace is another word for divine intervention - God's involvement in our lives.

TOO MUCH OF A GOOD THING
a story

The phone was ringing, or was that just part of his dream? He wasn't sure. Images faded to impressions as he floated up to the surface of consciousness. Just before breaking the surface and taking in that much needed breath, a final powerful impression threatened to keep him under. Something about it made him want to stay beneath the surface to see what it was. It was knowledge, and it's promise of enlightenment was powerfully seductive. He fought to stay under - kicking and paddling downward, but it was no use. The phone rang again and he surfaced.

He reached up, knocking over the glass that held the remnants of warm milk with a table spoon of nutmeg, and turned the tiny knob between his thumb and forefinger. He felt the heat on his hand and the light that burst out from underneath the lampshade violently forced his eyes shut. The phone rang again. With one eye closed and one eye alternating between squinting and closing he looked at the clock. It was 3:21 a.m. The phone rang again. It reverberated through his head like sounds in a gymnasium. He reached for the phone, then stopped, cleared his throat, and picked it up.

In his *trying to sound awake* voice, he said, "Hello." His mouth was dry and his speech thick and slurred. He had been asleep and he wasn't fooling anyone.

"Dad, it's me, Mike. I'm in a spot and I need your help," Mike, his only son said loudly, his voice far too casual for the state of their relationship. He was without inhibitions and his dad knew why.

"Where are you? What can I do?" shot out of his mouth like missiles.

"County D. And dad, hurry. I can't take it too much longer in here."

"I'll be there in twenty-three minutes. Hang on son, I coming," he said, his voice and his body now wide awake.

He jumped into the clothes that were draped over a wingback chair less than five feet from his bed. He thought of how if his wife were still alive the clothes would not be on the chair at all, and not because she would have removed them either. After dressing, he whisked down the stairs foregoing the brushing of teeth and hair. As he passed the mirror hanging in the foyer, he caught a glimpse of himself. He was a sight, not unlike that of his father the one night he had to come and bail him out of detox. His hair was disheveled and sticking up in the back. His eyes were red and there was sleep still hanging on at the corner of one, and there was a small drool residue extending from the right corner of his mouth to about an inch and a half up his cheek.

Continuing to the car he recalled how human his dad had looked that night so long ago. His dad, a stern, punitive patriarch, had never so much as had to have a parent-teacher conference on his behalf, so calling him from the county's DUI cell was the most horrific thing he had ever had to do. To his utter shock, his dad rushed down, bailed him out, and apologized for being so hard on him all the time. He said that he understood his son's need to let off a little steam now and again, just don't let it get out of hand. From that moment until this, he never had again. His dad's amazing grace had saved his life, for he had been taking a turn down the wrong path.

Driving toward the county courthouse, he thought about how that one incident with his father had destined how he had fathered his Mike. He was not the hard killjoy man his father had been. All of his days he was a father like his father was on that one fateful day. He was loving and merciful with Mike like few fathers had ever been. He had shown, daily, every bit of the amazing grace that his dad did on that one day, without ever seeing a response in his son similar to the one he had experienced. All of his efforts seemed to have been wasted on Mike, and yet on his ninth visit to County D in as many months, he was just as determined to continue those efforts.

"I knew you'd come," Mike shouted when his dad arrived at the officer's desk near the holding cell. Mike was leaning on the door of the cell and to say those four words caused him to lose his balance. He swaggered a little and then caught himself on the bars but not before banging into them hard.

"Can I help you, sir?" the officer at the desk asked in a nasal voice. The officer was a white female under thirty with jet black hair and dark colored freckles to match.

"Yes, my name is Harry Young, I'm here to pick up my son Mike."

"Sir," the woman said, her voice sounding even more nasal than before, "it would be better to take care of this in the morning.

"No son of mine is spending the night in *this* place," he said, his voice full of determination - enough to convince the officer that he was leaving with his son anyway, which, he did.

"Thanks, dad, you're the greatest," Mike said when they were in the car. His wry smile making him look like a youngster having just gotten caught with his hand in the cookie jar, or more likely in this case, looking up a little girl's dress.

"Son, I think we need to talk," Harry said.

"No sermons, dad, please," he said, his tongue thick and his speech slurred, but only slightly.

"No sermons. It's just that I want you to seriously consider moving back home," he said and before he had finished Mike was shaking his head from side to side. "Just for a while, son. I think it'd do us both some good."

"I am twenty six years old. I am not moving back into my parents' house. My dad's house," he said a tinge of sadness in his voice. He suddenly sat up, his movements exaggerated and clumsy, to look out his window, "Dad," he said in exasperation, "you missed my street."

"Don't you want to come home, at least for tonight. You can get cleaned up, have a good hot meal, and a good night's sleep."

"I can't. I have people waiting on me at my place - friends, you know. I can't let them down." He could tell his dad was disappointed. "They're good people, dad. They'll look out for me. I'll be okay. I'll come over and see you tomorrow, okay?"

"Okay," his dad said knowing that he wouldn't see his son the following day. And, he didn't.

"I could really use a little money, dad," he said before disembarking from the car.

Harry reached in his pocket and fished out a twenty

and gave it to his son.

"Is that all you have on you?"

He went fishing again. This time he caught a fifty.

"Thanks, dad, you're a class act -the best!"

The phone was ringing or was it? He wasn't sure. He was in a deep sleep, the likes of which he almost never experienced since his wife's death. He thought he would ignore it and then he thought about Mike. He bolted upright and grabbed the phone without so much as turning on the light. "Hello," he yelled, his heart racing, his head a swirl of conflicting thoughts and images. The voice was unfamiliar.

He arose, switched on the lamp, and sat on the edge of the bed starring at the floor. It had been only four weeks since his last late night call from Mike. Four long weeks in which he had not heard a word from Mike. He stumbled to the chair that had at least three outfits draped over it and began to get dressed. He tried, but he was unable to make himself hurry. He felt as if gravity was at five times its normal strength.

After finally managing to get dressed, he lumbered down the hall to the bathroom. He looked at his watch on the way, it was 2:32 a.m. In the bathroom he stared long and hard at himself, in particular the lines on his face, which were becoming increasingly more noticeable. He then washed his face, brushed his teeth, and combed his hair.

On the drive over, he began to think about how he had failed with Mike. He lamented about how his approach had not produced the desired effect in Mike's life. For the first time in his life he considered that there might have been a better approach. He thought about what approach he should take. What is more powerful than grace? There is nothing he thought. Then why was this happening? Wasn't grace enough? Mike had received grace and gotten the worse for it.

Just before reaching his destination, he determined that grace could be abused like anything else. His son had abused his grace, and he had aided him in doing so by continuing to give him more of it. His thoughts began to turn toward how he could change this. He would no longer give him grace and allow him to cheapen it. He would no longer insulate him from the consequences of his actions. He would change and then his son might actually change, too. But then, as he parked the car, he remembered it was too late.

In side the building he was escorted down a flight of stairs and through a long dark corridor, at the end of which, was his son. He was led through the large metal door and greeted by the officer as it slammed shut behind him. The sound jarred him, if only momentarily, out of his trance. After producing the necessary ID he was led over to where his son was. The man in the green outfit reached over and pulled back the sterile blue sheet. Mike starred up blankly, his eyes, long since lifeless, seemed to say, "I knew you would come for me, dad." And, he had. But, it was too late.

ns IS SIN
WHEN GRACE IS SIN

In the same manner that sin can become an opportunity for grace, grace can also become an opportunity for sin. Grace responds to sin with love, compassion, and forgiveness. It could be argued that if someone receives these things when they sin, they are likely to do it again. And, indeed this abuse of grace occurs quite frequently. Thus, an obvious risk is involved when grace is extended.

Grace and sin are bound together, existing in the enigma of a paradox. Thus, paradoxically, where sin abounds, grace abounds all the more, and where grace abounds, sin has the opportunity to reappear again. Sin and grace coexist like yin and yang and like light and darkness.

When the apostle Paul writes that, "Where sin abounds, grace abounds all the more" he goes on then to ask the rhetorical question that logically follows, "Should we sin then, that grace might abound?" He answers his own question with a definitive GOD FORBID! However, the fact that he had to ask the questions shows the precarious relationship which exists between sin and grace.

Grace is that amazing thing which above all else has changed my life. I have broken the law that God laid down for me time and time again, and when he responded with grace rather than punishment, love rather than hate, I was changed. Thus, is the power of mercy. However, I have also witnessed occasions and even patterns in my life where because of grace I continued to sin.

I have received grace and responded with sin. I have been given the most precious gift that has ever been given and proven myself to be unworthy of it. I have abused the precious unmerited favor of God by using it for another occasion of sin so many times that I fear I may never do otherwise. Which leads me to this question. What causes grace to become sin?

Grace can become sin when it is given without balance and discipline. This first principle does not apply to our relationship with God, because God's grace is given in balance and with discipline. However, we, as flawed and imperfect human beings, do not always give the gift of grace in balance. We often give the gift of grace or withhold it because we do or do not feel like it. We give the gift of grace without being able to see with the perspective of God. We only see one side of the equation rather than the entirety of it.

When considering the first principle, it is of paramount importance that we address our approach to parenting. What determines the frequency and level of grace that we give our children? Do we have a balanced, God-inspired approach, or do we do it on a whim or the way we are feeling at the time? The simple fact is, we probably disperse grace in a manner similar to the way our parents did or in reaction to them, as in the case of the previous short story. This is almost always the case unless we've taken the time to explore the pros and cons of how our parents did it. This painful evaluation is extremely difficult, and many people never find the strength to do it. However, our children's view of God's grace will be directly affected by the way in which we, their first image of God, give to or withhold from them the gift of grace.

Grace becomes sin when we use absolution as another way to say that we got away with it, and subsequently repeat the deed. Grace is not given to enable us to continue in sin, but rather to stop us from it. Thus, grace is most perverted when it is used to facilitate habitual sinning. Of the many things that perpetuate sin, slow punishment and grace perverted are the two greatest offenders. Often, those who receive grace rather than punishment or death, begin to feel as if it is another way of God giving his stamp of approval. **Grace is not Lawlessness!**

This, above all things, makes for cheap grace.

Grace is made cheap the moment we forget the price God has paid for this costly gift. Grace is a gift freely given, but it is not a gift that is free. To make the gift of grace available, God killed Jesus. In the balanced economy of God, nothing is free. Therefore, in order for God to give to us the gift of grace, he has to pay for it. It is not free. Nothing is free. King David seemed to understand this principle most completely. This is exemplified by his declaration, "I would not offer God anything that cost me nothing." David said this in response to one of his subjects trying to give him something with which to sacrifice to God. However, David insisted on paying for it.

I've heard many critics of Christianity say how ridiculous the crucifixion seems to them. However, without it, Christianity becomes a cheap, shallow, and elaborate system of reassigning the blame for the wrong we do. The message of Christianity is not that we can get away with the sins we commit, but rather one of a precious and costly grace that involves great sacrifice on the part of the one giving the grace. Grace is costly for the giver and the receiver, and when this is forgotten, grace becomes sin.

Grace also becomes sin when it becomes expected and unappreciated. Grace, as a gift, comes to us at the will of the giver of that gift and not the receiver. Often you and I resemble spoiled children expecting the grace of God rather than realizing that it is his to give, and we can neither demand it nor do we deserve it. In the course of my lifetime I have received an abundance of grace from both my earthly and heavenly parents. This makes me extremely susceptible to expecting grace, and indeed, on many occasions I have been guilty of that very thing. I have been responsible for abusing the precious gift of grace by perverting it into sin when I have expected it and by not being truly grateful when I received it.

God's grace is so readily available to us that we must each guard against simply expecting it. When we get to the place where we expect grace when we sin, then we have caused grace to be an accessory to our sin. Believing that we are going to get away with our sin before we even commit it causes us to do it with far less trepidation than we ordinarily would. Grace is not another way of saying that it is okay to sin, but we often treat it as if it were. This is the worst form of perversion and sin there is. We are actually using God's solution for sin as the best reason to sin. God help us.

Grace also becomes sin when it is not received in fear and trembling and then responded to quickly. When we forget the sheer awesomeness of the gift that we are receiving from God, we are all the more likely to treat it as common. It is a part of our nature to treat diamonds better than we do marbles and gold better than steel. If we forget that we are actually receiving life from God then we are likely to treat our pearls like that which is fed to swine.

We also must act upon grace. Grace is a gift that demands action. Like most gifts that we are given, grace calls for a response. When we fail to respond to grace, we've prostituted it into sin. Grace calls for action on the part of the one receiving it. Grace is a gift to be acted upon. God gives us grace in order that it might cause change in the depths of who we are. When we realize that what we've done should cost us our very lives or the lives of those that we love. When God says, "I'll pay for it with my life rather than yours," it should cause us to respond to him the way in which we would to a fellow human being that just jumped into the river to save us from drowning.

By receiving the gift of grace, we become indebted to the giver of that grace. And, the giver of the amazing grace that we most need only asks us to respond in love and to do our part in not habitually repeating the same mistakes over and over again. Jesus said that the one who is forgiven the most will love the forgiver most. This should also be true of grace. Rather than coming to expect grace, we should so love the giver of grace that we commit ourselves to insuring that he never has to give us such a costly gift ever again.

Jesus also said that once we become the recipients of grace we must go forth and give it to others. This is the action of grace - allowing it to change us and going forth to give it to others who need it. He also indicated that if we refused to give others the gift of grace we have received that it would be taken away from us. Therefore, the way to receive grace is, paradoxically, to give it away.

Grace should never be used as a means to continue in sin. However, it is so closely related to sin and is responsible for freeing us from the ultimate penalty of sin - death, that we must vigilantly guard against perverting grace into the very thing that it comes to rid us of - sin. We must never forget that an occasion of sin can become and occasion of grace. However, we must also always remember that an occasion of grace can become an occasion of sin, defeating its power to save us.

**Why the Worst
SINNERS
Make the best
SAINTS**

Why do the worst sinners make the best saints? Why do the best saints make the worst sinners? It is because of the unique and paradoxical relationship that exists between grace and sin. The important thing for us to remember is that our lives can be filled with either sin or grace or, in most cases, both sin and grace - it's up to us. I say it's up to us, but the truth is, it is only partially up to us. We are going to sin - we are going to fall short - that's not up to us. However, what we do when we sin *is* up to us.

The worst sinners make the best saints because of the incredible power of God's most amazing grace. Those who are forgiven most are the very ones that love most. Those of us who realize just how desperately we need God's grace and that there's nothing we can do to obtain it are changed forever when God freely gives us his grace. Are you a dirty, rotten sinner like myself? Take heart! We have more opportunities than anyone to receive the life-changing power of God's grace. For, where sin abounds, grace abounds all the more!

Be warned, all you saints out there, lest you forget. Grace carries with it a responsibility. Don't allow your gift of grace to become expected or taken for granted. Don't abuse the sacred gift that you have been given, for in the moment you do, your occasion of grace will become for you another occasion of sin.

Coming in the Winter of 1996
(In time for Easter)

THE RESURRECTION
AND OTHER STORIES OF LOVE

By
Michael Lister

The Resurrection is a collection of fictional short stories and novellas written by Michael Lister. These are love stories that touch both the spirit and the soul. Filled with stories of passionate love - both divine and human, *The Resurrection* is for those who have come to realize that there is a truth that can only be revealed in story. Exciting, tender, human, and filled with faith, this book will warm the heart while it feeds the soul.

Reserve your copy today by calling 904-639-3700

To order additional copies of **Why the worst Sinners make the best Saints**, complete the order form below.

Ship to: (Please Print)

Name_____
Address_____
City, State, Zip_____

__copies of **Sinners and Saints**   @ $9.95 each $____
Postage and handling @ $1.50 first book and $.50 all others $____
                                    Total Enclosed $____

Make check payable to **ST. MATTHEW'S PRESS**
                     P.O. BOX 1130
                     WEWAHITCHKA, FL 32465

Or call: **904-639-3700**

Available now:

THE SONG OF SUFFERING
Meditations from Job
By
Michael Lister

THE SONG OF SUFFERING addresses the most fundamental of human dilemmas: life, death, God, suffering, evil, and many others. It is a book filled with devotions that give inspirational thoughts and practical insights into difficult issues. Filled with ancient wisdom and modern applications, it is a unique blend of the mystical with the practical in a powerful and poignant way. Instructive without being *preachy,* **The Song of Suffering** is for both doubters and believers.

Only $7.95 plus $1.50 shipping   Call today - 904-639-3700 or write to: St. Matthew's Press P.O. Box 1130 Wewahitchka, FL 32465

Coming in the Summer of 1996

INTRODUCTIONS TO GOD

By
Michael Lister

How well do you know God? Would you like to know God better? In his new work, Michael Lister takes us on a fascinating exploration of who God is. ***Introductions To God*** is a unique and honest look at the identity of God. At times surprising - even shocking, this delightful book will help you to know God better - more fully, and more intimately. See God in a whole new light - the light of illumination in ***Introductions To God***.

Send $8.95 plus $1.50 shipping to: **St. Matthew's Press**
P.O. Box 1130
Wewahitchka, FL 32465
(904) 639-3700